Attract Anything With Reiki

Daily Rituals For Advanced Manifesting

Ingrid Morgan

Introduction

One of the main reasons why people become interested in reiki is the fact that working with reiki helps us make our dreams and goals come true. Of course, in order to make our dreams come true, we need to first heal ourselves by dealing with our own subconscious fears and thinking patterns. It is a bit of a truism that we regard the world from own perspective. Everything we experience is coloured by the lens of our beliefs- which stem from past experiences, the opinions of others, and narratives that we have internalized from the media. The study of quantum mechanics has found that the presence of an observer changes the outcome of the experiment. In essence, our thoughts have a profound effect on our external realities. We see what we expect to see. And what we expect to see is based on both social conditioning as well as the previous patterns we have observed. Many psychologists now state that neurons that 'fire together wire together.' This means that we tend to think the same things we always do, simply because we always have. And because we are thinking the same thoughts, our realities seem both consistent and continuous. But if we were to shift the way we think about things, how quickly could reality morph to fit this new conception? Everything in our universe is made up of energy, and our thoughts are no different. By changing the energy that you put out, you can change the quality of the things, environments, circumstances, and relationships in your life. The law of attraction relies on the simple premise that we attract to us the circumstances, people and material objects that match our predominant mode of thought. It basically states that you get back what you put out.

Introduction

So, if you are constantly thinking positive, loving and abundant thoughts, you will get back a reality that mirrors this belief. Of course, spending most of your time thinking positively is easier said than done. And for a lot of people it isn't even necessarily thinking positively that is the difficult part. It's preventing low self-worth from creeping in, and ridding ourselves of limiting beliefs about what is possible for us that is the most challenging. Luckily, there are ways that reiki's spiritual force can help us manifest our dreams and goals far more easily than through brute force. When channeling reiki energy toward a future vision, the vibrational quality of reiki helps us attract situations, people, and opportunities that also carry that same vibration. As you practice reiki day after day, lucky breaks will occur and you'll be guided into situations that provide you with a better understanding of what is right for you to do. Sometimes you'll be guided to do things that seem difficult at first, but suddenly resources and people materialize to help you out. You'll find that you are growing and developing in ways that are exactly right for you and a deepening level of happiness will develop within you.

What Is The Law of Attraction?

So, what is the law of attraction anyways? This concept has become wildly popular in the last few decades, and promises riches and happiness beyond compare, all with little to no effort on the part of the practitioner. Wikipedia defines the law of attraction as: "the name given to the belief that 'like attracts like' and that by focusing on positive or negative thoughts, one can bring about positive or negative results." And that really does sum-up the concept, but is a bit too high-level to be useful. The idea that 'like attracts like' is just that- that you draw to you experiences and objects that reflect your dominant mode of thought. If you are perpetually happy, optimistic, enthusiastic…you probably find that good things are constantly happening to you. After all, you go looking for positive experiences and they seem to magically appear! The same thing goes if your dominant mindset is a negative one: if you are constantly complaining about how bad everything is….why would you be surprised when more bad news shows up, you are pulling it to you like a magnet. The thoughts you think act as a broadcast signal that tells the universe what you would like to experience. One of the overarching themes of the law of attraction is that you get what you think of most, and the universe is always delivering what you are asking for.The problem is, often we are thinking about (and thus asking for) are things we don't want! There is a saying among people who espouse this belief that 'you don't get what you want, you get what you 'are.' You may desperately want a million dollars (who doesn't) but if the vast majority of your thoughts reflect a concern over your lack of money, and a general belief that you will never receive this kind of wealth, well then, you won't.

What Is The Law of Attraction?

After all, you've been 'asking' for lack, and the universe has delivered! This phenomenon plays out across many aspects of our lives, where we accidentally attract precisely the exact opposite of what we wanted. Low self-worth and internalized narratives from others can keep us stuck in a mindset that undermines our dreams. The more we think about the worst-case scenario, the more it shows up, which keeps us thinking about all the things that are going wrong. Breaking the cycle is hard. And beating yourself up about it doesn't exactly help either. Over time we get used to being disappointed, and our belief in the law of attraction and positive change diminishes. After all, if things haven't changed yet, why would they at all? This type of thinking is described by Jean Paul Sartre, the French existentialist as 'sour grapes.' We strive for something, like some delicious grapes on a tree. But when they are out of our reach, we tell ourselves that they must be sour, and we didn't really want them anyways. But this form of cold-comfort distances us from our goals. The longer we think defeating thoughts, the more entrenched the become. The longer we inhabit roles we do not wish to play, the more real they become. The good news is that thoughts really do affect things, and while we can become trapped in a negative feedback loop, we can also harness positive feedback to create powerful momentum in our lives that helps us achieve our dreams.

Thoughts Become Things

Many people think of thoughts as just that. Intangible, fleeting ideas that, unless we act upon them, have no affect on our physical bodies nor on our realities. But the notion that 'thoughts become things' is being increasingly investigated, with the findings confirming that our thoughts have more of an impact than we'd previously understood. A study conducted at Harvard University found that mindfulness meditation changed the physical structure of participants brains. Those who underwent eight weeks of meditation training had increased cortical thickness in the hippocampus, which governs learning and memory. There were also decreases in brain cell volume in the amygdala, which is responsible for fear, anxiety, and stress. Not only were these findings confirmed by brain scans-participants also reported feeling much better. Another study out of UCLA observed that individuals who meditate had far 'younger' brains than those who do not.The participants who had been meditating for more that 20 sight, memory, physical characteristics that tend to do downhill as we age. When the men were tested after the study, most of them had improved in every category, including becoming more flexible.

Get Fit- Effortlessly

Many of us have internalized the narratives that we have been told about fitness and exercise. We count the number of calories going in, and obsess about the amount of calories we burn. Changing the way we think about exercise can have just as dramatic of an effect as actually exercising. The average hotel room attendant asked to participate in a short study was found to clean an average of 15 rooms each day, with each room taking somewhere between 20 and thirty minutes to clean. When these individuals were asked if they exercised, they all answered that they did not, even though the work they completed met the daily recommendation for exercise. The hotel attendants were split into two groups and monitored for four weeks. One group was told that their work provided the recommended amount of daily exercise, while the other group was not told this. The group told that their work met the daily exercise requirements lost weight, lost body fat, had changes indicated in their hip-to-waist ratios and had their systolic blood pressure drop. These changes occurred even though the hotel room attendants did not change their habits.

Thinking vs. Doing

In much the same way that being told that you are exercising has the ability to change your physical being, the act of visualizing yourself exercising has a similar effect. A study conducted at the Cleveland Clinic Foundation by exercise psychologist Guang Yue compared two groups of individuals. One group would actually go to the gym, while the other groups would exercise in the minds. The group that actually went to the gym had an increase in muscle mass of 30%, while the group that exercised mentally had an increase of 13.5%. Granted, those who actually attended the gym had better results, but a 13.5% increase in lean muscle mass attributed only to visualization is pretty good! Similarly, a study that looked at the brain patterns of weightlifters lifting hundreds of pounds compared them to lifters that only imagined themselves lifting weights. In some cases, the mental practices were almost as effective as physical practice, and both exercise and visualization were more effective than doing either alone. A study by Russian scientists found exactly this, and examined a series of four conditions under which athletes trained, consisting of both mental and physical preparation, and recorded their outcomes. The four arms of the experiment consisted of:

Group one: 100% physical training
Group two: 75% physical training, 25% mental training
Group three: 50% physical training, 50% mental training
Group four: 25% physical training, 75% mental training

Thinking vs. Doing

The fourth group performed the best, despite putting in what would be considered by most to be the least amount of effort. Visualization stimulates the same brain regions as would be lit up if we were actually performing the activity. Perhaps you have experienced this phenomenon yourself? Maybe you visualized playing in a game or a taking a test to find that the outcome mirrored your expectations.

The Tenuous Line Between Real and Imagined

An experiment at Harvard Medical School had two
groups practice a little five-finger piano exercise for
five days. One group would actually play the exercise,
while the other group would just think about doing so.
At the end of each day's practice session, both groups
sat beneath a coil of wire that sent a brief magnetic
pulse into the motor cortex of their brain. The
transcranial-magnetic-stimulation (TMS) test allows
scientists to infer the function of neurons just beneath
the coil. When the scientists compared the TMS data
on the two groups—those who actually played the
piano and those who only imagined doing so—they
deduced an amazing idea about the brain: the ability
of mere thought to alter the physical structure and
function of our gray matter. For what the TMS revealed
was that the region of motor cortex that controls the
piano-playing fingers also expanded in the brains of
volunteers who imagined playing the music—just as it
had in those who actually played it.

We Are Who We Pretend To Be

"We are what we pretend to be, so we must be careful about what we pretend to be."

- Kurt Vonnegut, Mother Night

Unlike stories of cleaning staff losing weight due to a shift in perspective, or older men growing young by imagining themselves in their prime, the Stanford Prison Experiment is not uplifing, but it does dramatically display how quickly humans adapt to the 'roles' they are assigned. In 1973, Philip Zimbardo and colleagues set out to investigate whether the brutality reported among guards in American prisons was due to the sadistic personalities of the guards or had more to do with the prison environment. To study the roles people play in prison situations, and the psychological effects of prison life, Zimbardo converted a basement of the Stanford University psychology building into a mock prison. Candidates for the study were given diagnostic interviews and personality tests to eliminate those with psychological problems, medical disabilities, or a history of crime or drug abuse. In the end, 24 men who were judged to be the most physically & mentally stable, the most mature, and the least involved in antisocial behaviors were chosen to participate. Participants were randomly assigned to either the role of prisoner or guard. The prisoners were treated from the outset like criminals, and were arrested at their own homes, without warning, and taken to the local police station to be fingerprinted, photographed and imprisoned.

We Are Who We Pretend To Be

In order for the experiment to feel real, the 'prisoners' were blindfolded and driven to the psychology department of Stanford University, where the basement had been set out as a prison, with barred doors and windows, bare walls and small cells. At which point the deindividuation process began. All of the prisoners were stripped naked upon arrival, deloused, had all their personal possessions removed and locked away, and were given prison clothes and bedding. They were issued a uniform, and referred to by number only. (If at this point you, as a reader, are questioning the morality of this experiment, you're not alone in that sentiment). Similarly, all guards were dressed in identical uniforms and they carried a whistle around their neck and carried a billy club. They also wore special sunglasses to make eye contact with prisoners impossible. Zimbardo observed the behavior of the prisoners and guards (as a researcher), and also acted as a prison warden. Within mere hours of the experiment beginning some guards began to harass prisoners. The prisoners were taunted with insults and petty orders, they were given pointless and boring tasks to accomplish, and were generally dehumanized. Push-ups were a common form of punishment imposed by the guards. One of the guards even stepped on the prisoners' backs while they did push-ups. The prisoners soon adopted prisoner-like behavior too. During the second day of the experiment, the prisoners removed their stocking caps, ripped off their numbers, and locked themselves inside the cells using their beds as barricades.

We Are Who We Pretend To Be

To retailiate, the guards called in reinforcements and the first shift volunteered to stay on duty. The guards used a fire extinguisher which shot a stream of skin-chilling carbon dioxide to force the prisoners away from the doors. Next, the guards broke into each cell, stripped the prisoners naked and took the beds out. The ringleaders of the rebellion were placed into solitary confinement. All of this took place on the second day of the experiment. The experiment was intended to run for a full two weeks, but on the sixth day it was terminated, due to the emotional breakdowns of prisoners, and excessive aggression of the guards. While this study (and the novel Mother Night) highlights the dark-side of becoming who we pretend to be, this psychological trick can clearly be harnessed for good. The more time you spend inhabiting your 'chosen' role, the less of an imposter you will be as time passes. Eventually, the life you pretend to have will be the life you actually do have, so the role you choose to inhabit is very important. Whether you decide to play-act as the owner of a flashy car, a successful artist, someone who lives a healthy lifestyle- these choices will shape who you become permanently (or until you method act another role).

Putting The Law of Attraction Into Action

While 'acting as-if' is an incredible technique for putting the law of attraction to work, there are many ways of manifesting what it is that you want. Essentially, there are only three basic steps to follow:

1. Ask: clearly as the universe for what you want
2. Believe: believe that the universe is delivering what you want
3. Receive: the most difficult step, where you allow the blessings you have asked for to materialize.

It seems so simple! And if it were that easy, there would be no need for this book to be written. However, steps two and three can be a bit trickier than they initially seem. The believe part of the equation can be very difficult, especially if constantly confronted by your current reality. This can raise doubts about when, or if, you will manifest your desires. We will touch more on the benefits of 'acting as-if' later, but establishing a firm believe that you will have (or even better, do have) your desires is a great way of transitioning from fantasy to reality. The doubts that creep-up that question whether this is possible are commonly referred to as 'resistance'. Resistance can also block us during the receiving mode, as this is the step where you need to feel in alignment with what you've asked for in order for your 'ask' to manifest.

Putting The Law Of Attraction Into Action

Resistance usually takes the form of subconscious fears and doubts. We often don't even realize they're there. They just anchor us to our current realities and prevent our desires from manifesting. They act as counter-intentions and the more attention and energy they are given, the father we move away from what we want. It isn't that the law of attraction isn't working. It's just that the universe is getting two different intentions to work on – what we want and what we're afraid of. Wherever you focus the most energy upon is what the law of attraction will create. So, if you're focusing on fears and doubt, sadly that is what you will manifest, and not what you truly desire. If you want to experience success with the law of attraction, resistance must be overcome.

Resistance

And the first part of overcoming resistance? Well, identifying it for one, and trying to hone which ideas or behaviours are most responsible for keeping us from manifesting. Many people experience resistance towards things they feel unworthy of receiving on some level. Or, we hold contradictory beliefs about what we think we want. Perhaps we want a promotion, but on some level know that it will mean more time away from family and friends. So, we may sabotage our career efforts in order to avoid the perceived consequences, without really knowing we're doing it. For better or for worse, the things we tell ourselves become entrenched as belief systems. Once we draw a conclusion about ourselves or the world, we tend to look for evidence that substantiates our belief, which further entrenches that idea. And you will find evidence, of course, until these ideas become truisms in your head. We all tend to carry a lot of baggage from our past- old tramas, shame and perceived failures have a tendancy to perpetuate themselves until we are able to rid ourselves of them. Identifying these beliefs is an important first step in releasing resistance. Of course, not all resistance comes up at the conscious level. Imagine for a moment that your greatest dream has come true. Change, even change for the better can be difficult. Sometimes, when we set an intention with our conscious mind, it is our subconscious mind that notices all the different ways things might change. Because we keep the awareness of the unintended outcomes at a subconscious level, we never deal with them at the conscious level. We try to think about our goal, and to feel great about it so as to match the vibration of what we want, but it is difficult to feel good and truly have faith when doubt and fear keeps popping up.

Resistance

The reason this affects our results with the law of attraction so powerfully is because the law of attraction can only deliver situations and experiences that align with our dominant focus. If we have a bunch of resistance clogging up our energetic 'signal' we are essentially telling the universe, "Please send me more of this aggravation." Perhaps you spend 30 minutes a day visualizing the money and freedom you wish to attract. During those 30 minutes, you are a deliberate creator! Your energetic "signal" to the universe is broadcasting exactly what you want, and you begin to draw it to you. However, if you spend the rest of each day feeling stressed by about life, you job, your body — you cannot allow for the blessings you desire to come into your life! Your focus on lack makes you incompatible with what you wish to manifest trying to attract. It doesn't mean you can't or won't make progress, but it will be slow and sporadic.

"There was only one catch and that was Catch-22, which specified that a concern for one's safety in the face of dangers that were real and immediate was the process of a rational mind. Orr was crazy and could be grounded. All he had to do was ask; and as soon as he did, he would no longer be crazy and would have to fly more missions. Orr would be crazy to fly more missions and sane if he didn't, but if he were sane he had to fly them. If he flew them he was crazy and didn't have to, but if he didn't want to he was sane and had to. Yossarian was moved very deeply by the absolute simplicity of this clause of Catch-22 and let out a respectful whistle." - Catch 22, Joseph Heller

Resistance

Strictly speaking, a "Catch-22" is "a problematic situation for which the only solution is blocked by a circumstance inherent in the problem itself. The term "Catch-22" is also used more broadly to mean a tricky problem or a no-win or absurd situation. So, in order to get what we want, we have to not want it at all? As mentioned above, when we approach manifestation from a place of 'lack' and 'want' we separate ourselves from our desires. It sounds absurdist, and a bit of a catch 22. And in some ways, it is. When we desperately want something, we tend to focus on how we don't not have what we want, keeping it at an increasing distance as we come to long for it more, and for our efforts are awarded more longing. The key is a light touch. To want something without attaching many of the negative emotions we come to associate with want. Children are a great example of this. They are told to write a letter to Santa, and that he will deliver what they want on Christmas. So, they write their letters, send them off, and without really questioning the logitics of how Santa visits every house, even those without chimneys, all on one night…..they expect their present to show up. They think about their new toys with joy and expectancy, not doubt and negative emotions. And most children, especially if they have received presents from Santa before, simply accept this system. And the analogy of expecting presents from Santa is apt, even for adults. The law of attraction encourages us dream and come to expect that the universe will deliver us our desires.

Resistance

The problem is, how do we get back to a state of joyful expectancy, when we wholeheartedly believed that we would receive what we have wished for, without creating blockages or resistance that separate us from our desires and their actualization? The receptive mode, also known as the flow or the vortex, is the primary mental and emotional state you'll want to hold whether you're trying to manifest something specific or just want to have a fun, relaxing day. Being in receptive mode basically means that you are in the 'zone' and feeling good as your day flows wonderfully around you.

Identify Resistance

It's important to identify resistance so that you can actively and mindfully work to change your thoughts, behaviours and emotions. Most of the time, we're not even aware of what thoughts we put out into the universe. We simply respond to things outside of ourselves–current events, the news, how people treat us, the stock market, how much money we're making, whether or not our favorite sports team wins–and then having a feeling that is either positive or negative. When you are simply responding unconsciously to what happens around you, we tend to stay 'stuck' in our current conditions. This is why most people's lives never seem to change very much. They get stuck in a repeating cycle of recreating the same reality over and over with the thoughts and emotions they are sending out. Identifying resistance can be hard, but there are some clues it leaves in it's wake. Identifying resistance is an important first step to overcoming it.

Some common hints at resistance are:

Avoiding joy- While it might sound absurd to think you could be avoiding joy, resisting opportunities for growth, positive change or advancement can be indicative of avoiding joy. Change can be scary, even it it ostensibly brings about the things we want.

Addictive patterns- It goes without saying that drugs, alcohol and food make this list. But addictive patterns can be anything we compulsively repeat even though it's self-destructive.

Identify Resistance

High levels of stress- Gravitating towards the types of situations that produce extreme stress can be a hint that we are sabotaging ourselves by staying distracted.

Procrastination- Resistance often makes itself known in lots of small behaviors that add up to avoiding real progress towards your goal. So, if you regularly find yourself doing chores instead of manifestation work, there's a good chance you're working with an internal block of some sort. Minimizing your goals. Minimizing our goals sends the signal that we're not really that serious about what wish to manifest.

Stop Resistance In It's Tracks

So, how on earth can you release this resistance and finally make better progress? What if I told you that there were many easy, fast, efficient ways to dissolve the resistance that is blocking your goodness from arriving? Once resistance is released you will be spending more and more of your time focused purely on those amazing life experiences you wish to attract, and they can manifest much more quickly and easily. Not one of us is immune to resistance. We all have it to some degree. It is keeping us stuck and unhappy while other people keep moving forward effortlessly - or it seems effortless, anyway. While there are any number of things that give rise to resistance, two of the major sources of resistance are our self-worth, and the strength of our beliefs (and what we believe, of course).

Stop Resistance In It's Tracks

So, how on earth can you release this resistance and
finally make better progress? What if I told you that
there were many easy, fast, efficient ways to dissolve
the resistance that is blocking your goodness from
arriving? Once resistance is released you will be
spending more and more of your time focused purely
on those amazing life experiences you wish to attract,
and they can manifest much more quickly and easily.
Not one of us is immune to resistance. We all have it to
some degree. It is keeping us stuck and unhappy while
other people keep moving forward effortlessly - or it
seems effortless, anyway. While there are any number
of things that give rise to resistance, two of the major
sources of resistance are our self-worth, and the
strength of our beliefs (and what we believe, of course).

Self-Worth

Self-worth is the value we assign ourselves, but is importantly it is how we communicate to the universe what we believe we deserve to receive back. Our self-worth develops from subconscious programming we experience when we are young. Any pain, shame, abandonment, trauma, etc that we faced can create a loop of low self worth that further builds the foundation of our subconscious self-worth, thus affecting what we attract into our lives. So when our self-worth is low we are telling the universe that we aren't worth anything and therefore....dun...dun dun....nothing will come! In order to receive from the universe, you must first believe you will receive what you are asking for, and a big part of that belief is believing that you deserve to be happy and have your wishes fulfilled.

Belief

Belief in general is the crucial bridge between 'asking' for and 'receiving' what you want. If you want to successfully manifest things into your life, you have to be confident that what you want to manifest will manifest. Belief is the most important principle – if you don't believe in your power to use the law of attraction to manifest what you desire, then no positive affirmation, no focusing, no amount of action will make it happen. It all comes from you, from your mind and your readiness to change your thoughts and your life to suit your needs. What we get in life is controlled almost entirely by what we believe is possible for ourselves. Sure, wemay believe that it is possible to make millions of dollars playing sports, or to have a loving marriage, or be in great shape well into our advanced years. But although we may believe that these things are possible conceptually, if we don't believe that they are possible for us, we can't achieve them.

Quantum Manifesting

Everything Is Energy

Tackling limiting beliefs and low self-worth can be a difficult task. Citing positive affirmations doesn't work if you don't believe them. And while making a concerted effort to think positively is certainly a great start, the examples of older men 'growing young' and housekeeping staff becoming fit stemmed from a profound shift in beliefs. Luckily, while it may seem like a massive task to break the habit of being ourselves, the universe is on our side, and all positive changes create momentum in the right direction.

The Universe Has Your Back

Quantum physics deals with the tiniest particles of energy called quanta (that's the plural of quantum in Latin). Quantum physics is a nifty little branch of science to investigate if you're looking to firm-up your belief in the law of attraction. Quantum entanglement is often used to describe how the law of attraction works. While I suspect that this might be a bit of an oversimplification, I do think it is an interesting and empowering metaphysical viewpoint. Specifically the theories of quantum entanglement and the 'collapse of the wave function'. The collapse of the wave function refers to the fact that light and matter do not exist until something happens to make them 'real' with this something being the act of observation. Prior to observation, a wave function contains all of the possible outcomes of a particular situation, but only one appears in the real world when it is collapsed by being observed.

Quantum Manifesting

We really do manifest our realities! The next chapter will cover more about how the wave function works wonder for our ability to manifest, but it is far from the only physical phenomenon that 'influences' our ability to deliberately create our desired circumstances. On a basic level, quantum entanglement refers to two bodies that interact with each other, and become 'entangled' with one another. Photons are tiny little packets of light, and have a twin photon that they exists with in the universe. No matter how great the distance that separates them, their actions mirror one another. The state of one photon cannot be described without describing the other, since the actions of one affect the other. If you believe that the universe as we know it was created from a big bang, then all of the energy that is out there, that creates everything we see and know, stemmed from one source. Which means that everything is entangled with, well, everything. And since all things are connected with each other, if we influence one thing, we can influence another. What we can fully influence is the thoughts we have. Using our thoughts we can attract to us the people, circumstances, objects that we want to influence. All of those studies about how thoughts affect things? You can chalk it up to physics.

Quantum Manifesting

Neurons That Fire Together, Wire Together

"More times than I can remember I look around and I ask why the hole I'm in looks so strangely familiar. Probably because it looks a whole lot like all the other ones I dug before I got around to digging this one."
- Craig D. Lounsbrough

And while we're using a basic model of quantum physics to substantiate our beliefs about conscious creation, the 'collapse of the wave function' as mentioned earlier is a very empowering concept for re-aligning your thoughts towards the reality of your choosing. A lot of resistance comes up from our conception of the past. Perhaps something didn't work out for us as planned, so we consider ourselves to be a failure. Then we hold this thought repeatedly, which continues to create that future, creating more 'failure' and continuing to entrench our previous convictions. We begin to hold thought patterns for so long that to think anything other than what we have convinced ourselves becomes both difficult and uncomfortable. So if our minds create our reality, why does everything we wish to change seem so stubbornly persistant? Quite simply, neurons that fire together wire together. Our brain cells communicate with one another through chemical signalling–one brain cell releases a neurotransmitter that the next brain cell absorbs. When brain cells communicate frequently, the connection between them strengthens. Messages that repeatedly travel the same pathway in the brain begin to transmit faster and faster.

Quantum Manifesting

With enough repetition, they become automatic. That's what contributes to 'muscle memory' in sports and with musical instruments–with enough practice, we switch to auto-pilot. Of course, as previous chapters has alluded, the practice can often be only mental, with the only muscle involved in the practice of our craft being the one inside our head. One study investigating the effects of only mental practice on musical performance had volunteers play a simple sequence of piano notes each day for five consecutive days. Their brains were scanned each day in the region connected to the finger muscles. Another set of volunteers were asked to imagine playing the notes instead, also having their brains scanned each day. The brain scans revealed no difference between groups. Really, your brain doesn't distinguish real from imaginary! Humans evolved with a stress response that would give us the ability to fight or flee when faced with danger. Chemicals including cortisol and adrenalin to help kick start the body, pushing blood towards the major muscles to give you strength. Unfortunately , the exact same stress response kicks in when we imagine danger. The same hormones are produced regardless of whether the danger is real or imagined. What we imagine to be happening is actually happening as far as our brains are concerned. That's one of the reasons negative thoughts are so damaging. Stress hormones are created, neural pathways are reinforced, and our belief systems become more and more entrenched. Psychologists have long known that negative thought processes follow this same pattern– the more we "ruminate" on a negative thought, the more cemented the thought becomes.

Quantum Manifesting

Negative and traumatic thoughts also tend to "loop"– they play themselves over and over until you do something consciously to stop them. This is why thoughts that cause depression, anxiety, panic, obsessions, and compulsions can become so difficult to combat.

Healing Past Timelines

"The past, like the future, is indefinite and exists only as a spectrum of possibilities." -Stephen Hawking

By healing our past, we can change our future, which paradoxically (and to our benefit) changes our past too. That of course sounds very convoluted, so we'll go back to quantum physics to substantiate this theory. There is mounting evidence to suggest that the universe evolves backwards, with the starting event back-filled based on the outcome that resulted from it. Quantum physics tells us that objects exist in a suspended physical state until observed, when they collapse to just one outcome — we don't know what will happen until we investigate, and our investigation influences that reality. Whether or not certain events may have happened some time ago, may not actually be determined until some time in your future — it may actually be contingent upon actions that have not yet taken place.

Quantum Manifesting

It sounds far-fetched, but more and more experiments are confirming that this may be how our universe 'works.' An experiment published in Science a couple of years ago saw scientists in France shoot particles of light (photons) into a measuring apparatus. The most astonishing part of the study was that is demonstrated that what the researchers did in the present retroactively changed the events of the past. True to the wave/particle duality, as the photons fired in the experiment passed a fork in the apparatus, they had to decide whether to behave like particles or waves when they hit a beam splitter. After the photons passed the fork an experimenter could randomly switch a second beam splitter on or off electronically. Whatever the observer determined to select actually determined what the particle did at the fork (which occured in the past). The Uncertainty Principle brought to light the fact that particles do not exist with definite physical properties until they are observed. Every particle has a range of possible physical states but it's not until the actual act of observation that it takes on defined properties. Until the present is determined, contingent upon observation, how can there be a past? If we comprehend the world as a state of mind, then if a tree falls in the forest, and there is no one around to hear it, not only did it not make a sound, but there was no tree to begin with. If you need furthur proof? Just when you thought quantum mechanics couldn't get any weirder, Eli Megidish and his collaborators at the Hebrew University of Jerusalem were the first to show entanglement between photons whose lifespans did not overlap at all.

Quantum Manifesting

First, they created an entangled pair of photons, '1-2'. Soon after, they measured the polarisation of photon 1 – thus 'killing' it. Photon 2 was sent on a wild goose chase while a new entangled pair, '3-4', was created. Photon 3 was then measured along with the itinerant photon 2 in such a way that the entanglement relation was 'swapped' from the old pairs ('1-2' and '3-4') onto the new '2-3' combo. Some time later, the polarisation of the lone survivor, photon 4, is measured, and the results are compared with those of the long-dead photon 1. The upshot? The data revealed the existence of quantum correlations between 'temporally nonlocal' photons 1 and 4. That is, entanglement can occur across two quantum systems that never coexisted. Megidish and his colleagues speculated on some rather spooky interpretations of their results. Perhaps the measurement of photon 1's polarisation somehow steers the future polarisation of 4, or the measurement of photon 4's polarisation at step V somehow rewrites the past polarisation state of photon 1. In both forward and backward directions, quantum correlations span the causal void between the death of one photon and the birth of the other.There is no single timekeeper for the Universe; precisely when something is occurring depends on your precise location relative to what you are observing, known as your frame of reference. Of course, everything we experience depends on our frame of reference, not only our perception of time.

Quantum Manifesting

It is simply a whirl of information occurring in ours minds. Existentialism posits that we take up the past in the present; namely, that our current worldview and disposition colours how we remember the past. The past is highly subjective- even our own memories are subjective. If you are currently a very happy adult, you will likely remember your childhood more fondly than if you are at present miserable. Space and time are simply the mind's tools for putting everything together. In the end, even Einstein admitted, that "People like us…know that the distinction between past, present and future is only a stubbornly persistent illusion." The reason that things seem to persist is that our patterns of thought persist, and this familiary of thought becomes our reality. But if we change our thoughts, we literally change our worlds. That's why 'feeling great' is so often touted in law of attraction communities- to have great things you must think great things, and it is much easier to do that in a great mood. The same strengthening of neural pathways occurs for positive thoughts too. You can become trapped in a 'positive-feedback' loop just as you can become trapped in a negative one. If you are clinging to past pain, associating new thoughts and feelings towards these events can release some of the resistance associated with them. The past is not as persistant as we think, so it's important to choose our perspectives wisely.

Quantum Manifesting

The Feeling Is The Secret

"Once you start deliberately offering thought, you access the energy that creates worlds."
- Abraham Hicks Law of Attraction

In order to deliberately create the reality we wish to live in, we have to control our thoughts. If we wish to live in a positive, upbeat reality, then our thoughts must mirror the type of life we wish to live. And to think positively, we must feel, well…..positive. The Feeling is the Secret is a seminal work in the field of Law of Attraction that was written by Neville Goddard. Have you ever wanted something so much you could practically "taste it" as the saying goes? Perhaps it was a tangible item— such as a new shoes, a new car —or a desired experience –such as a new job or a wonderful vacation. Thinking about having this just feels great. Without realizing it, you set in motion the Law of Attraction to bring this into your life.When you did this, you were likely in a high vibrational state, and on the same 'frequency' of what it is that you desired. Unfortunately, most of the time our old training kicks in and we convince ourselves we'll never get what we want or that we'd better plan on settling for something less instead. This can be why we often get things we don't really want, as we don't sabotage our manifesting with doubt and fear. We just think…."wouldn't it be nice to own that" - and it shows up! If you want to change the kind of results your get in your life, the process starts with imagining what you want, and feeling amazing about it.

Quantum Manifesting

From that mode of excitement, gratitude and joy you will enter the 'receiving mode'—and begin attracting the "how to" steps to take. People that can help you get what you want will show up in your life, special deals will suddenly appear, all sort of positive coincidences will align. When you wake up every morning, your priority should be to start feeling good and to get that momentum rolling. Decide that for today, you're not going to worry about how things will show up, you're just going to go with the flow. Resolve to care more about feeling good than about what you think of your situation. Resolve to look at everything in the most empowering light possible. One of the first steps you can take towards manifesting your goals is to take the pressure off. A big component of successful manifestation is to believe that you will receive the outcome you desire. If you wanted to manifest more money into your life because money was very tight, would you believe that you could manifest 5 million dollars in the next month? You would probably want to believe that you'd believe, but it is a bit of a stretch goal to say the least. It would probably be a lot easier to start with an extra 50 dollars in the first week. Once you've successfully manifested an extra 50 dollars, it would be much easier to believe that you could do 100 dollars the next week. After all, you are now the type of person that receives more money each week.

Quantum Manifesting

Remember, there's no pressure in successful manifestations-ever. Have fun with it! There is a lot of talk concerning one's 'vibration' among those who believe in The Law of Attraction. Much like the atoms in a table vibrate at a certain frequency, so too does everything and everyone. To attract what you want, you need to be at the same vibration of what it is you are trying to attract, as 'like attracts like.'

Because Everything Is Energy, We Should Harness It

Albert Einstein called quantum physics "spooky action at a distance" and this is a very apt description of quantum entanglement. Groups of atoms can interact with each other, even when separated by great distances. Both reiki and the law of attraction are concerned with cultivating and maintaining, and harnessing positive energy. The law of attraction focuses on keeping your thoughts, (which are energy) positive and solution-oriented.To attract what you want, you need to be at the same vibration of what it is you are trying to attract, as 'like attracts like.' Luckily, reiki can help cultivate and maintain a high vibration, and gently clear away the mental blocks that keep us stuck. The Hon Sha Ze Sho Nen reiki symbol (which we will learn about later) is amazing for clearing past traumas and timelines, and is a fantastic tool for combatting resistance.

What Is Reiki?

Reiki is a spiritual healing art that relies on the subtle manipulation of energy by harnassing a universal life force. That 'force' that Yoda told Luke Skywalker about? Yep, it's basically the same thing. There is energy, or 'chi' all around us; everything we see and touch is made-up of vibrating particles. Reiki is just one of many practices that seeks to harness this energy and direct it to the intended purpose of the practitioner/Jedi. The word reiki comes from the Japanese word Rei which means 'Universal Life' and Ki which means 'Energy.' Reiki practitioners understand that everyone has the ability to connect with their own healing energy and use it to help both themselves others. Our body is composed of physical elements such as muscles, bones, nerves, arteries, organs, glands, etc. However, we also have a subtle energy system through which our lif- force energy flows. This system is composed of energy 'bodies' which surround our physical body and assist us in processing our thoughts and emotions. The energy bodies have centers called chakras, which work somewhat like valves to allow life force to circulate through our physical, mental, emotional and spiritual bodies. If our life-force is low or blocked, we are more likely to get sick, and when it is high and free flowing, we more easily maintain health and a feeling of well-being. One thing that disrupts and weakens the flow of life-force energy is stress. Stress is often caused by conflicting thoughts and feelings that get lodged in one's subtle energy system. These include fear, worry, doubt, anger, anxiety, etc. They are what contribute to resistance with the law of attraction.

What Is Reiki?

Continual stress can block the body's natural ability to repair, regenerate and protect itself so much so that the American Institute of Stress estimates that 75%-95% of all visits to doctors are the results of reaction to stress. The effects of unreleased stress range from minor aches to major health concerns, such as heart disease, digestive disorders, respiratory and skin problems. Reiki aids the body in releasing stress and tension by creating deep relaxation. Because of this, reiki promotes healing and health. The reiki system of healing is a technique for transmitting this subtle energy to yourself and others through the hands and into other natural phenomenon. Reiki restores energy balance and vitality by relieving the physical and emotional effects of unreleased stress. It gently and effectively opens blocked chakras, clearing the energy bodies and leaving one feeling relaxed and at peace. It also, importantly, can pave the way to more successful manifestations if you've found yourself unable to clear resistance in the past. Anyone can learn to tap into an unlimited supply of life-force energy to improve health and enhance the quality of life. Some reiki practitioners will use crystals and chakra healing wands as they find these can enable healing or protect a home from negative energy. Reiki works with the law of attraction to help you raise the energy you transmit so you can attract what you want into your life. Since everything in the universe is energy, harnessing energy to direct it towards your goals will greatly increase the speed and success of your results.

How Reiki Assists With The Law Of Attraction

To have success with the law of attraction you must complete the three basic steps that comprise it in sequence: ask, believe, receive. Any of the reiki rituals listed in this book will help with all three steps; including taking action in your waking life towards your goals. We'll touch more on 'taking action' in the next section of this book. For now, it is important to understand how reiki can assist in you in manifesting your manifesting journey so that you feel inspired to keep it up as often as your are able. The whole process should be joyous and whimsical.

Ask

Getting very clear about what you want is helpful as it is very difficult to manifest something you're not entirely sure you want. It is nearly impossible to get what you want if you don't even know what it is you want. So, visualizing in meticulous detail is very beneficial as it help you clearly 'ask' the universe for what you want.

How Reiki Assists With The Law Of Attraction

Believe

Reiki exercises are helpful with getting your mind to believe that you will manifest what you are visualizing. So often manifestations are killed-off before they even start owing to resistance. We may try to make a conscious effort to think positively and tell ourselves that we deserve what we are trying to attract. However, the conscious and subconscious mind, especially if it has been wired to be overly critical, can sabotage our efforts. Participating in these reiki rituals tells your brain that you are doing something to achieve your goals, in addition to gently ridding the mind and body of negativity.

Receive

Taking action towards you goals has not been covered at length but it is a very important part of the process for establishing belief. As much as many of us want to believe you can 'get something for nothing' it is a hard belief to establish. So much of what we learn is based on the theory of cause and efffect. If you do A, then B happens. If you work-out, you'll build muscle mass. If you go to college and study hard, then you'll get a good job. While there are of course exceptions to both of these examples, it is hard to undo years of social conditioning in one fell swoop.

How Reiki Assists With The Law Of Attraction

Taking action bypasses this belief hiccup as you are working towards your goal. Since we become who we pretend to be, taking action also helps establish us in our new 'role'- whether that be fitness buff, entreprenuer, parent or whatever it is that you desire. The actions needen't be arduous and difficult- even a few minutes a day spent cultivating reiki energy can be paramount in establishing new patterns of thought. Keep in mind that any kind of manifestation technique/meditation or creative visualization is just a template or a thought-form that gives you a chance to interact with your higher levels of consciousness more effectively. You can adapt any of these rituals and make them your own, adding them into existing practices, or stringing together elements that resonate with you most.

Reiki and Crystals

Combining reiki energy with crystals is a powerful technique for healing your physical, emotional and spiritual body as crystals speed-up the healing process. Crystals carry certain energies and when they interact with our chakras they can have a positive impact on boosting our well-being and harmonising our energies. Using crystal healing stones when performing reiki creates an amazing synergy of energy! It is believed that the interaction between the stones and chakras will return the chakra into a healthy vibration, therefore healing the part of the body affected more effectively. Here are a few healing crystals and their properties, although there are many other crystals not listed that you may wish to explore.

Amethyst

Amethyst is a great stone for helping to ward off negative energy. It has a relaxing, calming property to it so it's great for using before bed. Amethyst crystals work with the third eye and crown chakra to help the mind generate insightful solutions to problems.

Reiki and Crystals

Pyrite

Commonly known as "Fool's Gold" for its resemblance to real gold, pyrite is a metaphysical work horse. It is most commonly used for attracting wealth and abundance, and is also believed to hold a strong protective energy.

Rose Quartz

Rose quartz is often used by those hoping to attract love, or to strengthen existing relationships. Rose quartz allows its user to tap into universal love energy, so it's great for promoting self-love too.

Sunstone

Sunstone promotes creativity and vitality. It nourishes the sacral and solar plexus chakras to breed confidence, power and leadership.

Smoky Quartz

Smoky quartz helps you to overcome negative emotions such as stress, jealousy, fear, anger, and even feelings of depression.

Reiki Symbols

While the use of crystals in a reiki healing session is an optional but welcome addition, the use of reiki symbols is far more central. Reiki symbols are used in the practice of usui reiki, and allow the practitioner access to reiki energy when performing healings and in the attunement process. The reiki symbols act as a kind of bridge which connects the practitioner to certain vibrational states, with each state having a specific purpose. Learning the symbols is more than just learning how to draw the lines and speaking the words- it's about learning how to connect to the vibrational state represented by the symbol, and to invoke its presence. As certain symbols unlock specific energetic forms, it's best to use the correct symbol for the given task at hand. Reiki provides symbols for physical, mental/emotional and spiritual issues. The attunement ceremony is the way reiki masters teach their students the connection between the symbol and its essential symbolic meaning. In theory, without receiving a reiki attunement, the symbol is just a picture, but once one is attuned and draws the symbol while intending to connect with its energy vibrational state, they too can access that energy.

Cho Ku Rei

Cho Ku Rei is the Japanese name for the reiki power symbol. It is useful for all kinds of things, including increasing the power of one's intentions, accelerating healing, providing protection and most importantly for our purposes…manifestation. Cho Ku Rei, or the power symbol, generally means "place the power of the universe here." This symbol can be used at any time, but is great for during creative visualization and manifestation practices as it can be used to instantly boost your abilities. To draw this symbol, take your dominant hand and trace out the image below according to the numbers. You will first swip your hand to the right, then straight down, then wind your hand in an inward circular motion to create the coil. The coil-like structure of this symbol is incredibly telling. The coil can expand and contract to regulate the chi energy and can also be used as a funnel of sorts to intensify and focus power or to decrease and release energy when used in reverse. The coil can also be used to close a space around the receiver or an area in order to block out negative energies and to keep energies received from leaving.

Sei Hei Ki

The Sei Hei Ki symbol connotes harmony. The symbol resembles a wave washing across a beach or the wing of a bird in flight, and it is drawn with a sweeping gesture. Its intention is purification, and it is used for mental and emotional healing. Practitioners may use this intention during treatments for addiction or depression in order to restore the body's spiritual equilibrium, to help people recover from past trauma or to unblock creative energies.

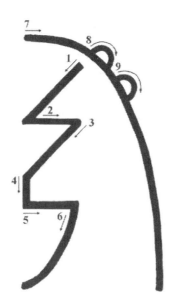

Hon Sha Ze Sho Nen

Hon Sha Ze Sho Nen is the reiki symbol used when sending energy across long distances. Its intention is timelessness, and it is often used to bring people together across space and time. Hon sha ze sho nen is also said to unlock the Akashic records, which some practitioners believe to be the source of all human consciousness. This symbol is useful for healing karmic ties, and traumatic past experiences. It is more than a little bit complicated to draw, so you may want to practice drawing this symbol many times before acting from memory. You can draw a large symbol (with the paint-by-numbers instruction) on a piece of paper and practice making the motion with your hand overtop of the diagram.

Raku

The Raku symbol is used during the final stage of the reiki attunement process. It is said to represent the chi or the life-force energy that runs down the spine through the chakras. Its intention is grounding. Practitioners use this symbol as the reiki treatment is drawing to a close, settling the body and sealing the awakened chi within. The striking lightning bolt symbol made by the hands is drawn in a downward gesture, symbolizing the completion of the healing session. This symbol is also used to separate the energy of the student and of the master after the attunement process is complete. Raku has a beautiful healing energy that can be used for removing kidney stones and blood clots. It can be imagined in pink or violet colour and acts as a laser for the affected area or the spot. It can be also used to remove blood clots from one's body.

Chakras, Reiki And The Law of Attraction

One of the main reasons why people become interested in reiki is the fact that working with reiki helps make our dreams come true. Of course, pursuing one's dreams and goals will still take a lot of time and effort, even with the law of attraction. The first thing, the need for patience, is important, because in order to make our dreams come true, we need to heal ourselves, first. And that requires dealing with our own subconscious fears and thinking patterns. But there are ways that reiki's spiritual force can help us manifest our dreams and goals far more easily than through brute force. Reiki energy carries the essence and vibration of love. When channeling reiki energy toward a future vision, the vibrational quality of Reiki helps to attract situations, people, and opportunities to us that also carry that same vibration. Just as we must let go of the outcome when giving a reiki healing, in manifestation, we must do the same. Holding onto and becoming invested in our vision in a needy, or rigid manner means that we are operating from a level of fear, which will only create more situations where our fears are triggered. In order to proceed and use reiki for healing and manifestation, we must first have at least a rudimentary understanding of the chakra system.

Chakras, Reiki And The Law of Attraction

Chakras

Odds are, if you've attended a yoga class or group meditation, your instructor most likely spoke about your chakras. But what are chakras, really? 'Chakra' is a Sanskrit word that means wheel. These centers were named as such because of the circular shape to the energy centers which exist in the energetic counterpart to our physical body. Using reiki to cultivate energy is very beneficial to your health and manifestation practice, but it needs a place to land. Your chakras are like little batteries that store and distribute energy throughout your body. There are seven main chakras and they are located along the spine extending out the front and back of the body. Each chakra has a number of specific qualities that correspond to the refinement of energy from the base-level of material-self identity, which is located at the first chakra, up to the higher-level awareness of being at our crown chakra. The chakras are formed at the junction of three connected energy shafts that ascend the spine, with the main column that runs up the spine being the Shushumna. The two lesser channels of energy — the Pingala on the right and Ida on the left — run parallel to the spinal cord. Chakras both take-up and collect chi (life-force energy) and transform and pass on energy. Our chakras serve as gateways for the flow of energy and life into our physical bodies. Every chakra corresponds to a specific aspect of human behavior and development. Our circular spirals of energy differ in size and activity from person to person.

Chakras, Reiki And The Law of Attraction

They vibrate at different levels relative to the awareness of the individual and their ability to integrate the characteristics of each chakra into their daily lives. The lower chakras are associated with fundamental emotions and needs: the energy at these chakras vibrates at a lower frequency and is therefore denser in nature. The finer energies of the upper chakras corresponds to our higher mental and spiritual aspirations and faculties. The openness and flow of energy through our chakras determines our state of health and balance. Each center has an integral function in creating our energetic balance. It is through the study of our energetic and physical being that we can create health, emotional stability and spiritual bliss. By drawing additional chi into our chakras, we can not only heal ourselves of previous thought pattens and behaviours that may no longer serve us, but charge ourselves up for greater and more rapid manifestation.

Chakras And Manifesting

If we visualize universal energy or chi as a current, our manifestations start at the crown chakra, our center of wisdom and spiritual connection. The crown chakra, our highest chakra, represents our ability to be fully connected spiritually. When we fully open our crown chakras, we're thought to access a higher consciousness. This is where the universe may start dropping us hints about the path we want to walk in this life.

Chakras, Reiki And The Law of Attraction

As that current moves down to the third eye, we start to engage with it and ruminate upon it. The third eye chakra speaks to our ability to see the big picture and connect to intuition. This is why clear thoughts and intentions are an important part of the process. The current of chi keeps moving down into our throat as we start to express our desires. The throat chakra gives voice to the heart chakra and controls our ability to communicate. When it's functioning at full capacity, it allows us to express ourselves truly and clearly. The more truthful we are with our expression, the more energy we infuse into the current of manifestation as minimizing our dreams prevents them from taking hold. The current then flows into our heart chakra, and as we hold the desire for our manifestation in our heart chakra it begins to be a part of our relationships. The heart chakra is one of the most important chakras since it connects the bottom three chakras (associated with materiality) with the top three ones (associated with spirituality). As the name suggests, this chakra can influence our ability to give and receive love—from others and ourselves. When our heart chakra is functioning optimally, we can network, find the right tribe, and feel the emotions that inform us about our journey.

Chakras, Reiki And The Law of Attraction

As the current ignites in the solar plexus, we start to take actions that back-up the desire we are trying to manifest.An open sacral chakra also governs creativity and sexual energy, as well as our sense of abundance,well-being, and pleasure. The last step is grounding our manifestations into reality with the help of the root chakra. The root chakra represents our foundation; it anchors us and gives us the feeling of being grounded. When the root chakra is open, we feel confident in our ability to withstand challenges and stand on our own two feet. Once this chi is at our root chakra, we build structure and routines around it to keep it strong. Having balanced chakras assists greatly with our manifestation process, and speeds-up the process of actualizing our dreams.

How To Self-Initiate

There are many reiki practitioners who insist that you absolutely must be initiated into reiki by a reiki master in order to be able to practice reiki yourself. While a reiki attunement or initiation is very beneficial, it is a bit elitist and exclusionary to insist that only those who can afford and access this treatment receive it's benefits. Of course, it is best if you can see someone with reiki training and practice to guide you on your journey. But if you are unable to receive an attunement from a reiki master, you can 'self-initiate' and do your own attunement, which will allow you to practice reiki and receive its healing benefits. Doing the attunement more than once is useful as a new initiate you'll need to practice before you get comfortable working with energy if you are new to the process. Many people misunderstand what the reiki attunement is. The most common belief is that the reiki attunement opens up the energy channels and connects a person with the energy source.

How To Self-Initiate

A reiki attunement simply reveals the energy potential, and establishes a direct connection between a person and the primary source of reiki such that people who have received the initiation become themselves a source of reiki. The healing process that the attunement initiates is the process of your energy bodies cleansing. Every person will feel it in different ways as it can take place physically, emotionally, mentally, or any combination thereof. Admittedly, the cleansing process can be rather unpleasant as physical conditions can temporarily get worse. Most often, in the course of this cleansing, the immunity of the person decreases, and there is an exacerbation of chronic diseases and increased emotionality during this time. If you're still game, you can see a reiki practitioner for an attunement, or you may 'self-initiate.'

Self-Attunement

It is our higher self that manifest things, but it still needs to be guided through our lower self – the subconscious mind. Reiki can help to heal the subconscious mind and provide increased energy to the higher mind- energy that can be guided towards manifesting your goals. As you heal your life through various reiki techniques, the amount of energy you can use increases greatly. To begin a self-attunement, or to give yourself a reiki session, you'll need to use the reiki symbols outlined in the previous chapters. The second reiki symbol, Sei Hei Ki, can be used to connect with your subconscious mind. And the third reiki symbol, Hon Sha Ze Sho Nen, can be used to connect with your higher self. By using these two symbols, we can create a 'bridge' between these two layers of consciousness, which can be used both to self-initiate, and later can be used to speed up the process of manifestation during regular healing sessions. The technique of using the symbols for manifestation is quite simple **it you are 'self-initiating, then the manifestation you wish to achieve is your initiation into reiki.**

Self-Attunement

Define The Goal You Wish To Achieve

If you are giving yourself an attunement, that will be your goal. If you are using this practice after you have been attuned, then thick about your dream, goal, what do you want to have, own, experience?

Open Up For The Flow of Reiki

To begin any reiki practice, you must activate the energy within yourself. Close your eyes and take a few rounds of deep breaths. Imagine the crown of your head opening and a stream of healing white light flowing into the top of your head, into your heart, and out through your arms and hands. Ask to be filled with light where you need healing most. As you feel the flow of energy, continue to breathe, and if you find your mind gets busy or starts to question whether this is working, come back to your breath. Envision yourself as a vessel for healing. Then set an intention or prayer to receive healing of the highest good. If you giving yourself an attunement, imagine the healing energy that flows in from your crown chakra descending through your chakras, one by one, while citing the following **affirmations as you focus on clearing your chakras. To begin, start with your crown chakra and state:**

Self-Attunement

I trust my inner knowing to guide me through life, understanding that everything happens for a reason, and that what I do makes a difference. Next, bring your attention to your third eye chakra and say:

I see the solutions to situations in my life and make positive choices. I am the creator of my reality, and my dreams are coming true. Imagining the healing energy you're receiving flowing into your next chakra, you will clear your throat chakra by saying:

 It is now safe for me to express my feelings with confidence and to create the life I desire. The next chakra is the heart chakra, the mantra for which is: I am a divine being full of Love, and give and receive this love freely without restriction as love is the answer to everything. Next, you'll clear your solar plexus chakra with:

I am successful and confident and I release my creative energy into my reality, effortlessly! Your sacral chakra will come next with the affirmation:

I live in good health and with vitality, I am unafraid to be myself. Lastly, for your root chakra:

I am safe and secure in the world around me and have all my needs taken care of. I know that I am the creator of my reality.

Self-Attunement

When you have finished your affirmations, you will next visualize and activate in your mind the first reiki symbol, Cho Ku Rei, with an intention of opening the connection to your lower and higher selves. Next, visualize and activate in your mind the second reiki symbol, Sei Hei Ki, with an intention of connecting to your lower self. After that, you will visualize the third reiki symbol, Hon Sha Ze Sho Nen, with an intention of connecting to your higher self. Intend for reiki to flow Into your higher and lower selves, in accordance with the highest good of all that exists. Say what is it that you wish to achieve, have, or experience. Visualize this goal, whatever it is, and feel the emotions and gratitude you would feel if you already had it. Continue to contemplate the achievement of this goal for the next five minutes or so. Then, visualize the first reiki symbol (Cho Ku Rei) with an intention of sealing the goal's manifestation. The last step is to visualize the Raku symbol for grounding and to close off the flow of reiki. Now you're done. This technique should be used on regular basis, each day or maybe even few times a day if you feel it's necessary.

Reiki Manifesting Rituals

Manifestation Box

Now that you are familiar with how to open the flow of reiki, you can begin incorporating reiki symbols and practices into your manifestation exercises. The creation of a manifestation box is a fun way use reiki symbols to help actualize your wishes. The whole process has a magical and whimsical feeling to it, and in the end you are left with tangible 'proof' that the law of attraction is working in your favour. Everyone wants to manifest when they come to reiki, and the creation of a manifestation box is a great way to start. Essentially, you will be writing out what you want, putting this slip of paper in the box, and waiting for it to manifest. To begin, you'll need a box that you love. It doesn't have to be expensive, and it can easily be a box that was once the wrapping of something else that you have re-purposed. But the more you love it the better. You'll also want to find a place to keep your box, somewhere special, and where it can be seen everyday. Once you have your box, you'll need a clear idea of what it is that you first intend to manifest. Write this out on a slip of paper- try to be as specific as possible while also being concise. Fold your slip in half and draw the Cho Ku Rei symbol in ink on the back of the slip. You may also draw any other symbols you feel as relevant, such as Hon Sha Ze Sho Nen if you are trying to manifest love.

Manifestation Box

Place the intention slip into your manifestation box and close the lid. Over the lid, draw the Cho Ku Rei symbol in the air with your hand, summoning reiki energy as you do. Everyday, continue to draw this symbol over the lid while you wait for your wish to materialize. Perseverence is very important, and over time you will see things happening for you. When you wish manifests, take the slip out and give thanks for having it in your life. You may burn the slip, or keep it in a 'book/box of proof' to help bolster your conviction in the process. There are no hard and fast rules for manifesting, but I have found this way of doing it effective.

Crystal Grids

Reiki crystal grids are fantastic for powering-up any manifestation. Crystal and stone grids have been used for centuries for spiritual growth and healing. Stonehenge is an example of gridded stones used for spiritual purposes, although using crystals to manipulate energy is not confined to sacred sites. Electronics use quartz crystal to transmit energy (and information). The purpose of a reiki grid is also to transmit (and amplify) energy. When created and empowered with intention, each stone within the grid amplifies the qualities and energy of the other stones and helps create a vortex of energy.

How to Construct a Basic Quartz Grid

Establish Intention

It is important to establish what you intend your grid to assist you with before you begin. Grids may be established with the intention of helping a world situation, your job or career, a relationship, a specific health issue, for financial abundance, or anything else that you want help in manifesting. Before building the grid, set the intent that you wish to build the perfect grid to assist you in your distant healing work and that you are guided to select the right crystals for it.

Crystal Grids

Selecting Crystals for Your Grid

While some people have very specific ideas of the types of crystals that can be used to create your grid, I personally think that any crystals you own can be used for this purpose, whether they are tiny stones, large clusters or longer crystal points. It seems that the concensus for crystal grids is to use single terminated quartz for the six outer crystals. Of course, many people use eight crystals for the outer ring, as the number eight is auspicious in Chinese culture and numerology. So, it will always be a very personal choice as to how you design your grid. If you are new to working with crystals, I suggest that you begin by working with clear quartz, as it is sort of the 'jack-of-all-trades' crystal and will work for many purposes. However, once you have become practiced in building and using reiki crystal grids, you might want work coloured quartz or quartz-like crystals, such as pyrite, rose quartz, amethyst points, citrine, etc. For the central crystal, I suggest using a crystal you find special- for example a cluster, a sphere, a pyramid, or just something particularly meaningful to you. Of course, the purpose of your grid may dictate the centrestone, and if you are working with all quartz outer points, you can still use a coloured stone specific to your intention for your master crystal. When you set up your crystal grid, do so in a special space that is neat and tiny. Once you have created your grid it will only take a few minutes each day to maintain the energy.

Crystal Grids

Cleansing and Charging Your Crystals

Now that you have determined what you will be using your grid to assist with and selected it's crystals and location, it's time to cleanse and charge the crystals you will be using. When cleansing crystals, hold the focused intention that you are helping the crystal release any less-than-light energy and return to a purified state. This can be done by holding it under running water, by smudging with sage, by soaking the crystal in salt water (make sure that your cystal is not water soluble), by placing it in the sunlight (not for colored stones), or by clearing it with Reiki and/or prayer. You can also bury stones in dirt, or place them on top of large clusters of salt for extended periods to help cleanse them, or you can cleanse them with singing bowls or by chanting 'om.' Once they have been cleaned, you'll need to charge them for your intended purpose. To do this, hold your crystals one at a time and put all of the reiki symbols you intend to use into them by drawing the symbols over them with your hands. When doing so, send loving energy into them, intending to charge them and asking them to serve as channels for your manifestation. This can take anywhere from 2-15 minutes per crystal, depending on your guidance. After cleansing and charging the crystals, place them in formation.

Crystal Grids

Arranging Your Crystals

To begin, write out what it is that you intend to
manifest on a slip of paper. Write is out as though it
has already happened, and express gratitude for having
received it into your life. For example, if you wish to
manifest a new home, you might write out something
like, "I am so happy to be living in my dream home."
You can make it as specific as you wish, and the more
specific the better. Draw the Cho Ku Rei symbol on the
back of the intention slip. Place this intention slip
where the middle of your grid will be. Next, take your
master crystal in your hands and intend to have the full
power of the reiki flow through you as you empower
your grid to heal and manifest with divine love. Create
an affirmation to do this. The affirmation can be
something like: "I am empowering this grid with divine
healing love now." Place this stone on top of your
intention slip in the centre of where you grid will be.
While placing the centre stone on top of the intention
slip, visualize your wish as having happened.

Crystal Grids

To connect the grid lines of your outer crystals to the centre crystal, start by taking one of your outer crystal in your hand and pointing it toward the central crystal, holding it a few inches above the centre stone. When you feel the energy begin to flow, use that crystal to draw the Hon Sha Ze Sho Nen symbol above the centre crystal. Next, move that crystal to the outside, laying it on the ground. You will repeat this will all your outer (six) points, evenly spaced around the centre crystal. Continue your affirmations, and when you feel that you are finished, come back to the central crystal, letting a final burst of energy flow into the central crystal as you draw Cho Ku Rei over the grid to seal it.

Crystal Grids

Maintaining Your Crystal Grid

Once you have established your grid, you will still need to maintain by continuing to send your intentions to the grid. Charge and activate your crystals on a regular basis until your manifestation is completed. Take out your intention slip after accomplishing your wish and either burn it, or save it in a special box.

Reiki Prosperity Box

This reiki ritual is very similar to the manifestation box, although it will focus on financial abundance specifically. Additionally, instead out writing out your intention, you'll be curating small objects that represent wealth. Reiki prosperity boxes are a combination of feng shui, another energy practice. It's very much an oversimplification, but feng shui, or geomancy, is a metaphysical belief system originating out of China that aspires to harmonize individuals with their environment by taking advantage of energetic forces. Individuals who practice Feng Shui believe that tapping into good energy will improve your health, finances and general well-being. Feng shui, reiki and the law of attraction are concerned with cultivating and maintaining positive energy. The first part of this reiki ritual is creating a symbolic representation of what you want to manifest in your life. You can place any objects that represent wealth into the box, in any quantity. However, the below listed crystals (and their quantity) have been selected specifically for generating abundance. Additionally, the count of eight is powerful as the number eight represents prosperity and abundance. It is the symbol of infinity and attracts limitless possibilities.

Reiki Prosperity Box

Here are the materials you'll need to make your own reiki prosperity box.

- Small Box
- Large Bill
- Eight Coins
- Eight Crystals

(citrine, green aventurine, clear quartz) These eight crystals of the following combination or all of the same

- Citrine – a yellow stone that aids in manifestation and creation. It cleanses our aura of negative energy and grounds us.

- Aventurine – a green crystal that brings luck and optimism. This stone attracts wealth, opportunities and abundance. It also removes negative patterns giving us the confidence to transform our lives.

- Clear Quartz – a clear stone that cleanses, amplifies and heals. It enhances our communication, clarifies our thoughts and elevates our energy into the sixth and seventh chakras. This stone will assist in maintaining clarity in our intentions and strengthens them.

Reiki Prosperity Box

Activate Your Reiki Prosperity Box

Once you have placed all of the contents listed above in your reiki prosperity box, you'll activate your box by channeling reiki and drawing with your hand the Cho Ku Rei and Sei Hei Ki symbols in the air over top of your box. As you do, begin to visualize the prosperity to wish to manifest. Visualization is a powerful tool in the law of attraction. If you can see it, you can attract it into your life. Spend several minutes in this meditation. Once you are done, bring your hands into prayer position for the next step – expressing gratitude. Give thanks for what you do have in your life. Maintain your eyes closed and hands in prayer position. When you are done, seal the box with the Cho Ku Rei symbol and repeat this exercise daily for 21 days.

Reiki Manifestation Triangle

Another manifestation strategy that relies on reiki is the 'manifestation triangle.' It's a simple technique that you can use to help solidify your beliefs and get clear about what you want.

How To Construct The Triangle

On a large sheet of paper, draw a triangle.
Beside the left point, write your name.
Beside the right point, write out your goal.
For example - to own and live in my own house. Above the top point, write the outcome. The more specific you are the better as you are more likely to get exactly what you wish for. For example, write down the neighborhood in which you wish to live, the number of bedrooms, the number of bathrooms, and any features you'd like for your home to come with-like a fireplace or large backyard.

Reiki Manifestation Triangle

In the middle of the triangle, write -" I am now manifesting this or something even better for the highest good of all." You may also draw with your pen the symbols you wish to charge up your intention with in the centre of the triangle. The Cho-Ku-Rei symbol is a great one to use, but feel free to add whatever resonates with you and is specific to your manifestation. Review your triangle everday until your manifestation comes to pass. When you do, draw your reiki symbols over the triangle (in the air, with your hand) and read your outcome outloud. As you are reading your desired outcome and drawing reiki symbols in the air, visualize with as much emotion and focus as you are able that you now have this object or experience in your life. The final step is to give thanks and let it go, trusting that it is starting beginning to take shape in the energetic realm.

Water

Manifestation techniques involving water are great for a number of reasons, the first being that it is cheap and easy to get your hands on, the second being that we all need to drink water anyways. Although estimates vary, the human body is between 50-75% water, so when you drink water that has been charged with reiki, you activate your whole body with the intention you've embued it with. In simple terms, this technique adds a lot of power to your affirmations and helps to program your body for manifesting your wishes. It can really open up your inner wish manifesting abilities. You'll also stave off dehydration, which is responsible for a whole host of diseases. Whether you are a reiki practitioner or not, you can charge your water with loving and healing energy. This book will highlight a technique that uses only one glass of water, but if you are familiar with the very popular "two cup method" you can also add reiki charged water to your reality transurfing techniques too.

"Glass of Water"

To start, you will need a clean sheet of paper and a glass of water (preferably filtered water). On the piece of paper, write down the wish that you want to come true, and write it is the present tense as though it is already a part of your life. For example, if you want to attract a partner you could write something like: " I am so happy and grateful to be in a loving relationship and sharing my life with a partner who helps me realize my full potential. My life is filled with passion and romance."

Water

You'll make the affirmation your own of course, and there is plenty of inspiration online if you are having difficulty finding the right words. It isn't particularly important how it is phrased, as long as it is written in the present tense, and that you are expressing gratitude for receiving it. Once you have chosen your affirmation, write it down on the sheet of paper and place your glass of water on top of the sheet of paper with the affirmation. Next, place your hands in gassho (palms together in prayer position in the centre of your chest), or held open as if ready to receive a gift. Then, imagine a beautiful bright light shining down from the heavens, entering your crown chakra at the top of your head, and filling up your whole body. Now, as you breathe out, imagine this energy radiating out through your palms, and place your hands on or around the glass of water. State the affirmation silently in your mind and vividly visualize your affirmation while concentrating on sending your energy towards the water in the glass between your hands. The key is your intention and your ability to concentrate on the state of being described in your affirmation. Your energy flows where your attention goes. When you concentrate your energy on the glass of water while visualizing your wish and stating your affirmation, you are charging it with the thought-form of your wish. Water is a very powerful energy conductor. You can charge the water for as long as you feel comfortable. The length of time you give your water reiki will depend on your personal beliefs. When you feel your water is sufficiently charged, drink that glass of water.

Water

You can practice this manifestation technique every morning and/or every evening before you go to sleep. As you might already know, many doctors advice to drink at least one glass of water every morning after you wake up. If you have more than one wish that you want to come true, then use a separate glass for each wish and make sure that nobody drinks from the glass you are using for the technique. If you want to add even more power to this technique, write out the affirmation on the new moon and do it for the first two weeks. Around the full moon, you should already see if you are moving in the right direction towards manifestation of your wish.

Incorporating Reiki Into Your Routine

Reiki is a wonderful way to bring divine guidance into your life and to guide your manifesting process. You can incorporate reiki symbols into any of the manifesting techniques that you currently use, use the rituals outlined in this book, or practice reiki self-healing. You'll find that as you involve reiki into your routine, lucky breaks will occur and you'll be guided into situations with people or experiences that provide you with a better understanding of yourself and of what is right for you to do. Healing experiences will also take place that help you release or work through blocks to truly meaningful success. Sometimes you'll be guided to do things that seem difficult at first, but once you accept them and begin to do them, resources and people will be there to help you. You'll find that synchronicities begin to pop-up everywhere and you will find a deepening level of happiness will begin to develop within you.

Work Hard To Achieve Your Goal

Although reiki is incredibly powerful and can certainly play a huge role in allowing you to develop the life you've always wanted, you substantially increase your chances of success if you also make concrete steps towards your goals. Although it may seem like the least fun and interesting part of the process, taking action doesn't have to be a slog. It serves so many purposes too: helping us to affirm our beliefs, and keeping our minds focused on what we wish to manifest and in doing so re-wiring the brain for a new reality. Action has a powerful effect both on your energy and on your mindset.Without action, no matter how much time and effort you put into visualizing your success, all you'll ever be is a person with a dream. The universe needs a vehicle to give you what it is that you want. If you want to be the founder CEO of a successful company, but haven't established a company, it will be a very tricky manifestation to pull off. The same thing goes with being a famous concert pianist that doesn't own or has never played a piano. It just isn't going to happen. Even savants who can play the piano from virtually the first moment they touch the keys still own an instrument and practice. The action doesn't need to be boring and it doesn't need to suck-up hours of your day. But you must work with the universe to make your goal a reality, and the more action you take, the more believable your new reality becomes.

Work Hard To Achieve Your Goal

Visualization and internal work is integral to your success – in fact, law of attraction teachers Esther and Jerry Hicks often talk about how one hour spent on your inner journey has the same impact as seven hours of taking action in the outer world. But that doesn't mean you can ignore the action step altogether! If you want to achieve real and lasting success, creating balance between your inner and outer journey is essential. If you wander around feeling great all the time, thinking and believing that you will receive what you want, the right people and opportunities will just magically fall into place. Once you've done the inner work, the action work comes far more easily. Kaizen is the Japanese word for "improvement." It is often used as a concept in business, and the concept has become so popular that you can become certified in teaching businesses how kaizen can help them achieve their goals. The small-step work improvement approach was developed in the USA and instead of encouraging large, radical changes to achieve desired goals, these methods recommended that organizations introduce small improvements, preferably ones that could be implemented on the same day. The major reason for this shift was that during WWII there was neither the time nor resources for large and innovative changes in the production of war equipment. The essence of the approach came down to improving the use of the existing workforce and technologies.

Work Hard To Achieve Your Goal

We will be applying this concept to our manifestation process to make small, incremental changes that will solidify our belief that our manifestations will materialize, and allow us to play the role of who we wish to be. It's not hard to fathom that small changes would lead to great results overtime, especially if multiple small changes were being implemented. Einstein famously called compounding interest the most powerful force in the universe, and dubbed it the '8th wonder of the world.' Of course, the purpose of this book is not to focus on finances, although the concept is analagous for all things we wish to attract to us. Try to manifest small objects or insignificant things like symbols and signs. Little things that are of no consequence are often much easier to manifest and much more fun. At the same time, try to increase log all the things that you are manifesting into your experience. Did a song you were just humming come on the radio? You manifested that! What about getting a person you were thinking about to message you? Gather and mentally (or physically) log as many of these experiences as you can. The more evidence you compile, the more belief you will have in the process and in your abilities to create change.

Shortcuts and Opt Outs

In many cases, you don't want what you think you want, or at least, not entirely. This is great for creating short-cuts and opt-outs that too can speed-up your manifestation process. Money is often at the top of many people's manifestation wishlists. In spite of all the importance that we place on acquiring money it is important to remember that money does not have any real value. Money is just paper or digital blips in a computer. What we really want are the things that money can buy- freedom, security, material possessions and experiences. Of course, many of these things can be obtained in round-about ways that don't directly involve the exchange of money. While you are waiting for your outer reality to catch up with your dreams, you can begin to feel and experience many of the things you desire with a little creativity. If it's travel you desire, there are plenty of work-exchange and couch-surfing sites that can help you take-off before you might otherwise be able. Many credit card reward programs offer discounted or free flights. If you are able to 'hack' your way to a travel experience before you would otherwise have been able to, the next travel experience will be that musch easier to manifest. After all, you are a person that travels! It is much easier to believe that you can do something if you have already successfully pulled it off in the past. There are often other solutions to our problems, or ways to acquire what we want that we are unable to see when we are focused on lack. Reiki can help to facilitate a mindset that is primed for problem-solving and help us get what is in accordance with our highest good.

About The Author

Ingrid Morgan is a reiki master, hypnotherapist and, well an author. She enjoys cream with coffee, stalking eBay auctions and is more than a little obsessed with the law of attraction. As an avid reader of Law of Attraction books, her favourites include "The Feeling is the Secret" by Neville Goddard, "The Law of Attraction: The Basics of the Teachings of Abraham" by Ester and Jerry Hicks and of course, "The Secret" by Rhonda Byrne. In keeping, Ingrid is also passionate about health, wellness and finance. As an Aries, she has always been consumed with getting what she wants. She is committed to finding the fastest, most effective path from desire to actualization- and wants to help others do the same.

Additional Works

Practical Magik: Harness the Law of Attraction to
Achieve the Relationship of Your Dreams
https://www.amazon.com/dp/B083BTX4CY

The Clear Skin Solution: A Less-Is-More Approach For
Clear, Supple Skin
https://www.amazon.com/dp/B07TVGF6TG

The Collagen Secret: What It Is, Why You Need It, And
How It's 'The Fountain of Youth'
https://www.amazon.com/dp/B07TK31YJJ

Change Your Brain, Change Your Looks: A 21 Day Law of
Attraction Experiment To Help you Achieve the
Physical Appearance You've Always Dreamed Of
https://www.amazon.com/dp/B07VDB7X46

Change Your Brain, Change Your Bank Account: 22 Feng
Shui and Law of Attraction Exercises to Manifest More
Money https://www.amazon.com/dp/B07VV5NLBC

Zen and the Art of Weight Loss: How Simplified Habit-
Stacking Can Lead to Extrordinary Results
https://www.amazon.com/dp/B081BD6TDL

The Tao of Manifesting: Power-Up Your Intentions To
Manifest Instantly And Get What You Want Using The
Law Of Attraction
https://www.amazon.com/dp/B082VMTJQS

Printed in Great Britain
by Amazon

58774523R00050